Oh no, POEMS!!!

NOTHING BEATS A PIZZA

Written and illustrated
by Loris Lesynski

Wait a minute.
WAIT A MINUTE.
Maybe something GOOD
is in it!

Annick Press

Toronto • Vancouver • New York

For my sister Lena

Annick Press Ltd.

We acknowledge the support of the Canada Council for the Arts, the Ontario Arts Council, and the Government of Canada through the Book Publishing Industry Development Program (BPADP) for our publishing activities.

Cataloging in Publication Data

Lesynski, Loris
    Nothing beats a pizza

Poems.
ISBN 1-55037-701-9 (bound)
ISBN 1-55037-700-0 (pbk.)

I. Title.

PS8573.E79N67 2001   jC811'.54   C2001-930080-8
PZ7.L47No 2001

Distributed in Canada by:
Firefly Books Ltd.
3680 Victoria Park Ave.
Willowdale, ON
M2H 3K1

Published in the U.S.A. by:
Annick Press (U.S.) Ltd.

Distributed in the U.S.A. by:
Firefly Books (U.S.) Inc.
P.O. Box 1338
Ellicott Station
Buffalo, NY 14205

Printed and bound in Canada by Friesens, Altona, Manitoba.

The art in this book was rendered in colored pencil, watercolor, house paint, tomato sauce, eyeshadow, rubber stamp-pad ink, and ordinary pencil.

The text was typeset in Utopia and Syntax with some other fonts doing guest appearances. The ones that look like handwriting are called Lemonade and Zemke Hand. The title on the cover is in Klunder.

Write to Loris
at Annick Press,
15 Patricia Ave.,
Willowdale, Ontario
Canada
M2M 1H9

Visit us at:
www.annickpress.com

reading without pizzazz

reading out loud with pizzazz

INGREDIENTS

INTRO

A *picture* of a sandwich
    isn't really like a sandwich
        and you wouldn't feel too full
           when you were done.

A ball, if you just hold it,
    never threw it,
    never rolled it,
isn't really like a ball
that's any fun.

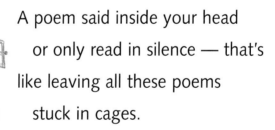

A poem said inside your head
    or only read in silence — that's
like leaving all these poems
    stuck in cages.

But **read aloud**, with noises,
    made by you, the girls and boyses —
then you'll hear them leap right off
    the pages.

Nothing Beat-beat-beats A Pizza

Nothing beats a pizza
when you're in a pizza mood
because a pizza isn't anything
like any other food
other food is neat and tidy
pizza's slippy pizza's slidey

*(makes me full and satisfied-y
nicest slices now inside me)*

Make a pizza
bake a pizza
take a pizza home
eat a pizza in a group or
on your own.

When we **want** to eat a pizza
then it's better having **two**
'cuz just one pizza's not enough
for me and you
and you
and you
and you and you and YOU.

Nothing Beats a Poem

Nothing beats a poem
when you're in a
poem mood because
you never know
exactly what a poem
might include.
It offers laughs
and often thoughts
and pictures in your head,
and sometimes says,
"Let's look at things this
other way instead."

Make a poem bake a poem
take a poem home
write a pizza poem
in a group or on your own.

Pizza's cheesy pizza's chewy
pizza's gooey pizza's good
(really slow beat)

Pizza'scheesypizza'schewypizza'sgooeypizza'sgood
(really fast beat)

5

Bizzy Boys

Busy boys are bumping thumping
   clumping down the halls.
Busy boys are stamping stomping
   tromping up the walls.
Yelling boys are making noises—
   don't get in the way!
And what are they so busy at?
   They're going out to play.

"Hey!" cried the buffalo.
  "What's that noise?
I think I heard
  a herd of boys!"

A Guy's Gotta Move

A guy's gotta move
  like he knows where to go
a guy's gotta move
with an ebb and a flow
a guy's gotta know
when to stand
when to glide
a guy's gotta know
  inside

Backwards Max

Backwards Max comes down the hall
    as fast and straight
    as a bowling ball
    but in *reverse*
and he stays upright!
    Did Max rehearse at home last night?
We have to laugh,
    though the teacher glares.
What's going to happen —
    what's going to happen —
    what's going to happen
when he hits the stairs?

Backwards Me, Backwards You

I write my name down backwards.
    Who would that person be?
Some other someone
    as totally different from me as
    you ever did see.

Write your own name backwards.
    Who would *that* person be?

loves writing
likes kids
afraid of mean dogs
laughs a lot
not very tidy
loves music

Loris Lesynski

wears icky colors
snarls a lot
extremely neat
likes turnip
sings on key
goes skydiving

Sirol Iksnysel

7

Too Many Amandas

On the very first day of school they came
    ta da
        ta da.
Twenty-one girls with the very same name
    ta da
        ta da.
They came in pairs up the halls and stairs,
they filled up most of the classroom chairs,
all of them saying the name was theirs,
     ta da   ta da
        ta da ta da ta da.

The teacher stared and had to hiss,
   "I've never had a class like this.
Amanda here, Amanda there.
   I see Amandas everywhere!"
Oh, when she goes to
   the class next door—
they have eleven Amandas more.

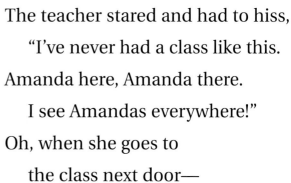

8

One Amanda

One Amanda,
   two Amanda,
      three Amanda, four.
Five Amandas come a-marching
 through the classroom door.
Six Amanda, seven Amanda,
   eight and nine and ten.
How will the rest of us *ever* remember
   which is which of them?
Tall Amanda,
   Math Amanda,
Amanda who lost her boot.
   Amanda with freckles, Amanda B.,
Amanda who plays the flute.
   Amanda who has a basset hound,
Amanda allergic to peas.
   Two Amandas who make us laugh,
and seven Amanda G's.

I Look in the Mirror

I look in the mirror
   and what do I see?
Someone that everyone else
   calls me.
This is my hair. This is my nose.
   These are my shoulders,
   and these are my clothes.
They see me, they know me,
   they call out my name.
They seem to believe that
   I'm always the same.
But none of my dreams or
   my thoughts can be seen.
You can see what I look like
   but not what I mean.
Look at me closely with
   all of your eyes —
   all you will see is
   my perfect disguise.

9

Pizza Theme & Variations

To fry up a frightful witches' pizza,
choose between spiders and bugs.
Melt eye of newt and
tongue of toad,
and sprinkle it with slugs.

A dragon can toss a pizza high
in the air with a flip of his tail,
cook it fast with a blast of flame,
and eat it with ginger ale.

You're fired!

Jack was a pizza delivery boy
till the day of the Giant's call.
Jack couldn't balance the "party size"
on a beanstalk quite so tall.

Porridge too hot?

Porridge too cold?

The story of Goldilocks *could*

be told

with pizza.

"Papa Bear's pizza?

Not enough cheese.

Mama's has too many

anchovies.

But Baby Bear's pizza?

The best in the wood!"

Said Goldie, "It's almost

un*bear*ably good

pizza."

Princesses' pizzas in days of old were royal circles of scarlet and gold.

Forsooth! My pizza doth be cold!

11

Pizza with
1 topping · 2 toppings · 3 toppings
or EVERYTHING

"Everything"

A pizza with "everything on it"?
I want it I want it I want it!
But I wonder . . . does "everything"
mean the same thing
to everyone else as me?

Choices

CRYSTAL BALL PAC

"Everything"?
Moon pizza sprinkled
with golden stars
and swirls of tomato-clouds
straight from Mars.

"Everything"?
May I suggest
mice
on every slice?

The candy-lover's
pizza wish?
Jelly beans,
chocolate,
and licorice.
"Everything"
is not complete
(sugar, more sugar!)
unless it's
sweet.

Oh, children......

Mock Pizza

Bet it's not
fantastic pizza.
Bet it's
tastes-like-plastic pizza.

Imitation mozzarella
   powdered pepperoni
the crust is just like cardboard so
   you know the dough is phony

fake salami
   oily sauce
      onions dehydrated
old tomatoes
   bacon bits
      cheese-like substance grated

    deep-dish pizza?
    cheap pizza
    cheddar pizza?
    cheater pizza

pizza-maker, what's the deal?
pizza-faker, make it real
    odd pizza?
    fraud pizza!
not-inside-**MY**-body pizza!

Mud pies, bro?

Mud pizzas,
to go!

Old, Cold Pizza

Old, cold pizza.

  Having breakfast all alone.

Everybody's gone to work.

  There's only me at home.

Wish that someone else was here.

  Pizza, could you say:

"Morning, kid — I hope you have

  a really awesome day."

Once Upon a Time-ee-o

Once upon a time-ee-o
  (begins this little rhyme-ee-o),
a mommio and daddio
  were all alone
  and sad-ee-o,
and so they thought
that maybe-o
  they'd have a little baby-o.

The baby-o was you-ee-o,
  their little honeydew-ee-o,
once so sweet and small-ee-o,
  but now so big and tall-ee-o.

And like the other kiddee-os,
  you're into sports and videos
and like to bike and race-ee-o
  and go from place to place-ee-o,
talk-talk-talk on the phone-ee-o
then read and be alone-ee-o
or hang out with the guys-ee-o.

But in your parents' eyes-ee-o
you're still their little bunny-ee-o,
  so even though it's funny-o,
just *let* them reminisce*-ee-o.
  (*And every once in a while-ee-o,*
  although it's juvenile-ee-o,
  but just to make them smile-ee-o,
  let 'em hug and kiss-ee-o.)

*REMINISCE (rem-i-**niss**) means when people go on and on about the past and how wonderful it was and how cute you were as a baby.

What I'd Like to Know

Do teachers ever giggle?

Do teachers ever drool?

Do teachers ever wish
they didn't have to
go to school?

Do teachers ever end up spending
recess all alone?

Do teachers ever miss me when
I'm sick and
staying home?

When teachers get together with
their friends at half past three,
do teachers have as good a time
as all my friends and me?

No Smirchling Allowed

A brand new teacher came today
  from one of the other schools.
"Be serious," she ordered us,
  "and listen to my rules.

"There won't be any splurching,
  and you're not allowed to flitz.
Anybody caught klumpeting
  will put me in a snitz.

"No floozering at recess.
  Grufflinking's not permitted.
And anyone who splubs outside
  will *not* be readmitted.

"When you put your hand up,
  I don't want to hear a bloud.

And let's be clear that while
  I'm here, no sneeping is allowed."

I was truly baffled, but I didn't
  want to show it.
What if I was flitchering and
  didn't even know it?

We sat as still as statues.
  None of us made a peep.
All of us were terrified
  we'd accidentally sneep.

We didn't have a *clue* about
  the rules that she was using.
How can anyone be good
  when being good is so confusing?

THE CLEAN DOG
Boogie

"Too messy!" said our mother
   when we asked her for a pet.
But then we saw a sign for one
   we knew she'd let us get:
"Guaranteed — the cleanest dog
   the world has ever known."
Just the pet we wanted!
   We had to take him home.

It started in the car: he tried to lick
   the windshield clean.
"What a helpful puppy," said our
   mother, "what a dream."
In the house, he polished all
   the doorknobs with his tongue,
then used his snout to vacuum, getting
   every single crumb.
He licked the dusty lampshades. He slurped the dirty walls.
   He chased the dusty bunnies up and down the dusty halls.
His ears were perfect dishrags, his tail a built-in broom.
   He soaked himself in soapsuds and he rolled around the room.

But then — he *ate* the lampshades,
  licked the photo albums blank.
Found the dish detergent,
  every drop of which he drank.
He swallowed up a scatter rug
  while lapping at the edge.
Books and houseplants toppled as
  he swept the window ledge.

"Take him out!" our mother said.
  We didn't question why.
He slobbered on the seesaw.
  He sucked the sandbox dry.
Then he licked the baby's head
  and made her even balder.
Where's the pet shop owner's card?
  Right away I called her.

Dog-lips cleaned the phone as I
  described the situation.
"Sort of an… experiment,"
  she said in explanation.
"But check his head: the seventh
  brownish freckle near the top—
that's the switch." I found it.
  Instantly, he stopped.

Once he was a cleaning machine,
  now he's a regular mutt.
We're delighted to have him the way
  he is, a conventional canine,
  BUT…
when my room gets dusty,
as it does every now and then,
  I'd almost like to find that switch
    and turn him on again.

Ruby

Ruby wakes up full of pounce
    and instantly begins to bounce:
playing catching growling chasing
    darting jumping running racing,
skittering up and down the halls,
    chewing shoes and bones and balls,
pretending a hat is an enemy rat,
    shaking it, making it ragged and flat.
    Then suddenly — down on the floor she'll plop,
no pause at all between GO and STOP,
    and right in the middle of a *yap-yap-yap*
she's sound asleep in an instant nap:
    that's what puppies do.

Sigh...lence

The foss…

    foss…

       faucet's

          dripping…

             *plink…plink…plink*ing in the sink…

and the kitchen clock is ticking … it's so quiet, who can think?

**I can only do my homework
when there's music noise and sound,
when there's barking boiling talking,
when the house is really rocking, for
my brain is trained to do its best
with racket all around!**

So now…

  how can…

    I concentrate…

on spelling or subtracting?

  This silent…

    peaceful…

      atmosphere…

        is *totally* distracting.

21

The Bad Mood Blues

You *wake* up in the morning and
you *know* it's there

BAD M O O O D

BAD M O O O D

From underneath the covers
you can feel it in the air

BAD M O O O D

BAD M O O O D

22

Everything goes wrong the day
you wake up in the dumps
you know your socks have vanished
and your hair has gone in clumps
      your milk is spilling everywhere
      your brother has to *poke* you
      and everybody's bugging you
      and says it's just a *joke,* you
          know it isn't fair and know
          you're totally upset
          and the *day* hasn't even
            the *day* hasn't even
            the *day* hasn't even

S   T   A   R   T   E   D   Y   E   T

so whatcha gonna do
when you wake up feeling blue
gotta figure out a way to
get a rhythm to the day

and B E A T B E A T B E A T

B E A T B E A T B E A T

B E A T B E A T B E A T the

BAD MOOD away.

Buster's Scat Singing

When you've got the mulligrubs
when you're feeling low
when you're just a sourpuss and
no one wants to know you
  you gotta have a place inside
that's always good to go to
somewhere down inside you where
you're happy smart and wise, and
there's dancing in the street, and
there's music in the skies
then instead of feeling draggy
feeling crabby, feeling glum,
you can rise above the grumbles
and have some fun.

Taste Buds

"WHAT'S IN YOUR MOUTH?" asks the substitute teacher.
Everyone's staring at Bonzo McFee.

Taste buds for sour
taste buds for sweet
taste buds for bitter things awful to eat
taste buds for salty
like popcorn and chips
waste buds when Brussels sprouts
cross your lips

He stops in the middle of chewing and answers
(ever so sweetly), "Well now, let me see:

> there are glands for saliva,
> there's all of my teeth,
> molars, incisors,
> with gums underneath.
> One epiglottis,
> one palate,
> one tongue.
> At the back of my throat there's
> a uvula hung.
> Over ten thousand taste buds
> and millions of cells.
> Is that what you wanted to know,
> Mrs. Wells?"

The regular teacher
  knows Bonzo loves gum.
And also smart answers.
  And playing dumb.
He wouldn't question. *He* wouldn't shout.
  He'd say very simply, "Spit *all* of it out."

We ♥ Sour!

Mike likes pickles
more than pie.
So do I. So do I.
Keeps sour candies
in good supply.
So do I. So do I.
Maybe our tongues
are missing some
of the taste buds meant
for candy and gum?
Lemons and onions
and relish and pickles,
green apples and
mustard —
yum!

Where does all the air inside the bubbles of my POP wallow when I swallow and the fizzing has to stop?

Lately I've Been Late

Lately I've been
late a lot.
Is this some *disease*
I've got?
I've become so
very
slow
just can't get myself
to go
want to wait
and want to stall
lots to look at
watch it all
clocks are ticking
everywhere
don't much notice
don't much care
sometimes time
is slow and sweet
I've got a case
of summer feet.

Cloud Pizza

Look, the clouds
are arranged today,
it seems to me,
in a pizza-shaped way,
but take a bite and
you'd have to say,
*"Sky pizza, air pizza,
tastes like nothing-there
pizza."*

Play Ball!

High ball, low ball, fast ball, slow ball, curve ball, swerve ball, straight ball, great ball!

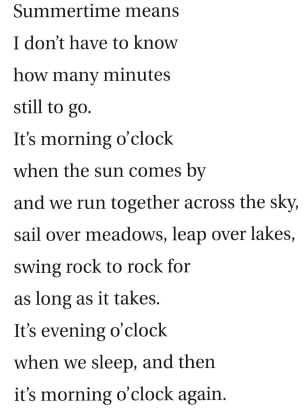

Morning O'Clock

Summertime means
I don't have to know
how many minutes
still to go.
It's morning o'clock
when the sun comes by
and we run together across the sky,
sail over meadows, leap over lakes,
swing rock to rock for
as long as it takes.
It's evening o'clock
when we sleep, and then
it's morning o'clock again.

Leaves

Leaves were here

they left their prints

in greenish grayish brownish tints

like rubber stamps along the road

an autumn message left in code

Pizzas were here.
They left their
crumbs...

28

No Two Snowflakes

No two snowflakes
are the same.
That's what gives them
all that fame.
But what about potatoes?
What about peas?
What about you's
and what about me's?
They're not identical.
They're not so similar.
Snowflakes aren't really more
incredible than these.

Snowman Pizza

Snowman pizza must have just
   a plain and simple ice cream crust
with snowflake sauce in an icy glop
   and grated icicle bits on top.
But this is one pizza you'd never bake.
   Imagine the size of the puddle you'd make!

No two pizzas
are the same...

How Sam Eats

Sam eats his sandwiches
all round the edges,
biting the sides away fast.
He says that the centers
are best in his
sandwiches.
That's why
he saves them
for last.

"It's not scientific.
It's all the same sandwich.
The middle is just like
the rest" —
that's what we all said
before we gave
sandwiches
Sam's Sandwich Center
Taste Test.

The pointy part of pizza
is the bit
that tastes the best.
I'll nibble
at the little tips
and you can eat
the rest.

You're driving me crazy!!!

Good Advice

Never **ever** sit beside
    a picky pizza eater.
They're always so suspicious, what
    they'll like and what they won't.
Finicky, they pull off bits
    not sure to be delicious.
And do they mind the choosing?
    No, they don't.

Never **ever** sit beside
    a picky poem writer.
They're always fussing with the words
    to make a poem brighter.
Adding here, erasing there, to get
    it right. They really care.
And will they ever bother less?
    They won't.

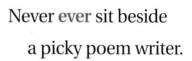

You're driving me crazy!!!

Dear Reader

If Nothing Beats A Pizza
makes you hungry for your own,
if you want to write a story,
if you want to write a poem,
then play with words and say with words
what's shaking in your mind.
Imagination makes the writing really fun to find.
Any idea begins it. Any idea can cook.
Now *go*, dear adorable reader —
you've come to the end of this book.

FOOTNOTES

Answers to the Most Frequently Asked Questions:

- Why "pizza"? The author admits that *she's*
  in love with *zzzz*-zy sounds like these.
  Enjoy these poems, but be on guard:
  your lips may fall off if you read them too hard.

- No, a poem does not *have to* rhyme to be a poem.

- Yes, there are more books like this in the works.

THE END